Your Identity in Christ

Andrew Wommack

Published in partnership between Andrew Wommack Ministries and Harrison House Publishers.

Woodland Park, CO 80863 – Shippensburg, PA 17257

ISBN 13 TP: 978-1-59548-637-0

ISBN 13 eBook: 978-1-6675-0461-2

For Worldwide Distribution, Printed in the USA

1 2 3 4 5 6 / 26 25 24 23

Contents

Introduction

I once heard about a man at an airport who was having trouble booking a flight. The airline worker behind the counter was doing everything she could to help this customer but was getting nowhere. To make matters worse, the line behind the man began to grow as people waited for their turn.

Eventually, the man—who must have been some sort of VIP—became so frustrated, he started yelling at her, "Do you know who I am? *Do you know who I am?*" The woman looked at the man for a moment, grabbed the public address microphone, and announced over the loudspeakers, "May I have everyone's attention? Does anyone know who this man is? Apparently, he's forgotten."

That's a funny story, but I think it really illustrates a valuable message. Have you become frustrated, waiting on God to do something—wondering if He really knows who you are? Have you struggled with feelings of unworthiness? Have you ever wondered exactly what it means to be a believer in Jesus Christ?

Well, if you're having a Christian identity crisis, the problem isn't with God. May I suggest that if you aren't seeing the Lord's very best in your life, it's because you don't know who you really are in Jesus Christ. Sad to say, the vast majority of people in the body of Christ don't know who they really are, and because of that, they are struggling to believe and receive what's available to them as a believer.

I want to share with you one of the key revelations that changed my life. When I learned about a believer's true identity in Jesus Christ, I became free to simply receive everything God had for me.

Knowing who you are in Jesus Christ is foundational for successfully living the Christian life. I believe that once you learn about these things, it will make a huge difference in your spiritual walk; and you'll begin to see God's promises manifest like never before. You'll be blessed!

My "Re-dedicator" Was Worn Out

For all have sinned, and come short of the glory of God.

Romans 3:23

One Sunday when I was eight years old, the pastor in my family's Baptist church preached a message titled "A Tour of Hell." It was very dramatic and gave us insight on the kinds of people who went to hell. The pastor didn't pull any punches and even named names of well-known people who had recently died.

He said there were not only thieves and murderers in hell, but he also talked about all the good people who were there. They lived relatively good lives but trusted in their own goodness instead of Jesus for their salvation. That sermon shook me to my core.

When I got home from church that morning, I asked my dad what the pastor was talking about. He explained what true salvation was, I prayed with him, and I got "born again." It happened right there in my bedroom with my dad! Praise God! *But then, I went back to church.*

I heard that to please God, I had to keep working to live a holy life, do all the right things, and avoid sin. I swallowed that kind of teaching—hook, line, and sinker. I may have never used profanity, but I would feel condemned if I just saw a profane word scribbled in a bathroom stall. I wouldn't even go swimming where there were girls present because my church called that "mixed bathing" (which, I guess, sounds much worse than "mixed swimming").

I was so sin conscious, it seemed like I re-dedicated myself at every church service. I'd respond to the altar call because of the sin I thought I had in my life. I did it so often, if there were such a thing as a "re-dedicator," mine would have been worn out!

I've never said a curse word, smoked a cigarette, or drank liquor. I've never even tasted coffee—not that I have anything against coffee. Mark 16:18 says you can drink any deadly thing, and it will not harm you; so you have a scripture for that, amen! My point is that I was living holier than most people have ever thought about. As a result, I became a modern-day Pharisee.

That all came to an end the night the Lord really touched my life on March 23, 1968. I was at a prayer meeting on a Saturday night in the youth pastor's office at our church. I won't go into all the details, but the Lord showed up. I saw my relative unworthiness in the face of God's true holiness, and I came up way short (Rom. 3:23).

In the wake of that experience, I turned myself inside out and began confessing every sin I ever committed—or even thought about committing! As I was lying there, in a puddle of tears, waiting for God to strike me dead because of my sin, something miraculous happened.

Renew Your Mind

And be not conformed to this world: but be ye transformed by the renewing of your mind, that ye may prove what is that good, and acceptable, and perfect, will of God.

Romans 12:2

The Lord had shown me my hypocrisy and self-righteousness—that all my good works were like filthy rags in His sight (Isa. 64:6). After an hour and a half of repenting, I waited to see what the Lord's response would be. But instead of rejection, I had the supernatural love of God just overwhelm me.

For over four months, I was caught up in the love of God. I knew that God loved me, but for the first time in my life, I knew it had nothing to do with my performance. He loved me because He was love, not because I was lovely. Although that experience was life changing, I still didn't understand how a Holy God could love someone like me. How could the Lord just overlook all my failures? I was confused.

Thankfully, I learned that all I had to do was sow the incorruptible seed of God's Word in me (1 Pet. 1:23), and it would do the rest. And that became the focus of my life. Over the next few years, I began to see what the Word had to say about who God really is and who believers are in Jesus Christ.

Since then, I've been renewing my mind to the Word of God day and night, and it has truly transformed my life (Rom. 12:2). I discovered why I could experience God's love so freely. And it ultimately led to the revelation of my true identity in Christ. (We'll come back to this story later!)

Learning who you are in Christ is simply renewing your mind to the truth of God's Word. Every truth the Lord has shown me over the years was already deposited in my born-again spirit but just had to be drawn out. It's like thirsting for life-giving water and leaning against a well. All you need to access it is something to draw out the water.

I began to see the truth about my identity in Christ while I was serving in the military during the Vietnam War. With all the sin and debauchery going on around me, I had no choice but to stick my nose in the Bible and study it—sometimes up to fifteen hours a day—every day for thirteen months. Now, I know that's not practical for everyone.

If you are a full-time student or a working parent with children, you can't just lock yourself away in a closet for fifteen hours and read the Bible. But you can take one scripture and meditate on it day and night (Josh. 1:8). For example, there was a time when I studied and meditated on Ephesians 4:17–24 for a whole year, and it changed my life! What I'm telling you is that you are never going to discover who you really are in Christ—you're never going to draw out what's deposited in your born-again spirit—until you renew your mind and become transformed by the Word of God.

There is security in knowing who you really are. That is the reason people are so reluctant to change. They are secure in what they know and very fearful about what they do not know. That's also why it's so important to renew your mind to God's Word regarding your identity in Christ.

A New Creature

Therefore if any man be *in Christ,* he is *a new creature: old things are passed away; behold, all things are become new.*

2 Corinthians 5:17

It is necessary that you know you are a new creature in your spirit! To think this way, you have to renew your mind to God's Word before you start seeing the perfect will of God made manifest in your life. You won't benefit from the truths found in the Word until you convince yourself of them (Col. 1:12; Philem. 6).

It's the same as if a person were a millionaire but couldn't benefit from their bank account because they didn't know the money was there. I believe this is the condition of the body of Christ. The vast majority of believers are simply ignorant of who they are in Jesus and of the rights and privileges they have in Him.

> There is security in knowing who you really are.

Another example of this in the natural is related to our freedoms as Americans. We've been endowed by our Creator with certain inalienable rights which are guaranteed to us by the governing documents of the United States of America. But citizens, especially Christians, have just become so passive that many of our rights have been trampled by ungodly leaders.

I remember during the 2020 COVID pandemic, the governor of Colorado put restrictions on places of worship. To be good neighbors, our ministry complied for a time. But once I learned that the governor had limits placed on his emergency powers, I notified him that our voluntary cooperation would end. We went through lawsuits, and there was even a point I thought I might be arrested just for hosting events at our Charis Bible College.

Eventually, the U.S. Supreme Court ruled in favor of churches over similar issues in other states. After that, the governor backed down. It was awesome! But that would have never happened if I didn't know my rights.

It's the same way in the spiritual realm. Many believers let the enemy push them around. They feel saved but stuck because they don't know their rights. We need to realize that we are totally dependent on Jesus, but we have to go beyond that and realize that as we depend on Jesus, we are totally superior to any weapon the devil can use against us. We are world overcomers (1 John 5:4). Hebrews 12:2 says we have to look unto Jesus, the author and finisher of our faith, but most of us have been looking at ourselves.

I'll tell you, if you don't know your identity in Christ, Satan is going to eat your lunch and pop the bag! Sad to say, there are many churches today that are not discipling people and showing them their true identity. That's just terrible!

"Old-Time Religion"

This is *the covenant that I will make with them after those days, saith the Lord, I will put my laws into their hearts, and in their minds will I write them; and their sins and iniquities will I remember no more. Now where remission of these* is, there is *no more offering for sin.*

Hebrews 10:16–18

Most Christians today aren't aware that their "old-time religion" is polluted with many traditions that void the power of God's Word. One of those traditions is that sin is still a barrier between them and God.

The Old Testament way of relating to God is not the same as the New Testament way of having a relationship with God. The Old Testament was legalistic and based on performance. You had to do certain things to get God's approval. The New Testament, on the other hand, is a covenant of grace based on acceptance of what Jesus already did. Because of that, there is a huge difference between the way people approached God under the Old Testament and the way they should now approach Him under the New Testament.

Under the Old Covenant, a sacrifice had to be offered every time a sin was committed. Then, once a year on the day of atonement, a sacrifice was made by the high priest for everyone and everything just in case something was missed. However, all these sacrifices were just types and shadows of the ultimate sacrifice—Jesus—that was to come (Heb. 9:8–12 and 24–28).

The Old Covenant way of thinking is still prevalent today in the body of Christ. Average Christians have been taught, and believe, that the sins they committed before they were born again were all forgiven the moment they were saved. But they also believe the sins they commit after their salvation all have to "come under the blood" and be confessed, one by one. This is why before my life-changing appointment with God, I felt like I constantly had to re-dedicate myself and tried to live the holiest life possible to please God.

An extreme legalist believes that if a Christian does not confess their sins, they will go straight to hell. The less extreme view is that, at the very least, a person will lose their fellowship with the Lord, and He will not answer their prayers. Both are wrong. If you have made Jesus your Lord, you've become a new creature, and sin is no longer an issue between you and God.

Don't misunderstand what I just said. Sin is still a factor, but it's not the Lord holding your sins against you. He placed all of your sins, past, present, and even future sins upon Jesus and He now deals with you through your faith in Jesus and what He did for you.

But sin gives Satan an inroad into your life. Romans 6:16 says that when you yield to sin, you yield to Satan—the author of that sin. And the devil only comes to steal, kill, and destroy (John 10:10). The Lord doesn't deal with you according to your sins, but Satan does. So, as much as possible, we need to quit sinning. And when we do, we need to repent and shut the door on the devil and the place we've given him in our life.

Sin doesn't change God's heart toward those who have received His salvation. But sin will change our hearts towards God. We need to keep a sensitive heart to the Lord and not be hardened through the deceitfulness of sin.

We have to be bold in our relationship with the Lord, but most Christians aren't. They approach God with fear of punishment and rejection. They fear they aren't worthy and that they haven't done enough to earn the right to be in His presence. They still believe their relationship with the Lord depends on their performance, and mixing the Old and the New Covenants makes the Word of God void in their lives.

We've got to believe that our identity is in Jesus Christ, through Him we have been made righteous, and we have unlimited access to God (Heb. 4:16)!

You're Not an "Ol' Sinner"

For he hath made him to be sin for us, who knew no sin; that we might be made the righteousness of God in him.

2 Corinthians 5:21

Have you ever heard someone say, "I'm just an ol' sinner, saved by grace"? That sounds humble, but it's just a product of wrong teaching and wrong believing about who we are in the spirit. Praise God, I *was* an "ol' sinner," but I got saved by grace. And now, I'm the righteousness of God in Christ Jesus. A born-again believer is now worthy in their spiritual man. Their spirit is righteous and truly holy!

Maybe you've heard somebody say things like, "All our righteousness is as filthy rags," and "There is no one righteous; no, not one." These statements are taken from scriptures (Isa. 64:6 and Rom. 3:10) that refer to our *self-righteousness*, which can

> We have to be bold in our relationship with the Lord.

never bring us into fellowship with God because *"all have sinned, and come short of the glory of God"* (Rom. 3:23). But Jesus took our sin and became sin for us so that we might be made the righteousness of God in Him (2 Cor. 5:21).

If you accept that Jesus became sin for us, then you have to accept that you have *His* righteousness in your born-again spirit. This is not righteousness imparted in heaven after you die. It will be perfected in heaven—spirit, soul, and glorified body. But, right now, in this life, your spirit is righteous and truly holy.

The spirit that you had, which was dead unto God, is gone. And the new spirit that you received at salvation is righteous, truly holy, and perfect—just as Jesus is. Your born-again spirit is actually the same spirit you will have throughout all eternity. It will not be changed or improved upon. One-third of you is now wall-to-wall Holy Spirit!

The rest of the Christian life—and most people's struggle—is bringing the soul and body in line with that truth. In Romans 12:2, the apostle Paul didn't pray that believers would receive something new from God but rather that they would renew their minds and prove (or make manifest to the physical senses) what was already there.

Healing, deliverance, prosperity, and every other good thing from God is already deposited in your born-again spirit. God did not change you only in principle at the new birth. You are now, in your spirit, a totally new creation. But until you first realize this and then act on it in faith, the devil will continue to oppress you.

Dead to Sin

Know ye not, that so many of us as were baptized into Jesus Christ were baptized into his death?

Romans 6:3

The most effective way the devil steals a Christian's rights is through religious unbelief, specifically teachings about us being unworthy and "ol' sinners saved by grace." Now, it is true that we were all born sinners (Ps. 51:5) and had the nature of the devil working in us (Eph. 2:2–3). But when you come to Christ and receive salvation, you become a new person in the spirit.

When you become born again, your body doesn't immediately change. For example, if you were a man before you accepted Christ, you'll still be a man afterward. And your soul—your mind, will, and emotions—didn't automatically change either. It's subject to change, but you have to renew your mind to experience salvation in your soul.

You become a brand-new creature in the spirit. Your spirit is made totally new. There isn't an old sin nature left in you. This may come as a shock to you if you were taught to believe that after salvation, you are still the same at your core—that you are still an ol' sinner.

But if you have been living your whole born-again life trying to restrain your old sin nature, it's because you've been led to believe you have two natures fighting against each other within you. And because of that, you've been missing out on all God has for you. That's almost schizophrenic, and it produces Christians who are nothing like Jesus.

The apostle Paul dealt with this issue in Romans 6 after proving in the preceding chapters that God deals with us by grace through faith. So, the logical question he knew people would ask was, *"Shall we continue in sin, that grace may abound?"* (Rom. 6:1).

Of course, this is not what Paul was saying. Instead, Paul responded with another question:

God forbid. How shall we, that are dead to sin, live any longer therein?

Romans 6:2

What a profound question to ask! Sadly, this is not a belief shared by many Christians today. They believe that they are still alive to sin and that it is with much effort, frustration, and failure that they battle their old sin nature the rest of their lives. But that's not what Paul believed. Paul went on to say that once we are baptized into Christ (Rom. 6:3), our old sin nature is dead. It's gone. It doesn't exist anymore.

Resurrection Life

For if we have been planted together in the likeness of his death, we shall be also in the likeness *of* his resurrection.

Romans 6:5

Maybe you're thinking, *What do you mean? I'm not dead to sin. I still struggle with many sins!* Now, I will admit that Christians still sin. **But our nature has been changed**; it's brand new. The only reason a person still sins is because they don't know this truth (John 8:32), and it's only the truth you know that sets you free.

> You become a brand-new creature in the spirit.

Think of it this way: our minds are similar to computers in the sense that they can be programmed, and they will continue to function that way until they are reprogrammed. We were all born in sin, and our old sin nature programmed our minds to be selfish, bitter, angry, lustful, and every other ungodly thing. But remember, when you are born again (John 3:3), you become totally new in your spirit. Your nature completely changes. It's not in the process of becoming new; it's already as pure and perfect as Jesus (1 John 4:17; 1 Cor. 6:17; and Eph. 4:24). That's your true identity!

Paul called this the "*likeness* of *his resurrection*" (Rom. 6:5). But, in order to fully experience it, he said we have to know that "*our old man is crucified with* [Jesus], *that the body of sin might be destroyed, that henceforth we should not serve sin*" (Rom. 6:6). He's talking about getting rid of your old identity. This isn't something that has yet to happen or happens over and over again; it's a done deal. In your new, born-again spirit, you are dead to sin.

Romans 6:7 says, "*For he that is dead is freed from sin*." But there is a difference between being freed and being free. During the American Civil War in 1863, President Abraham Lincoln issued the *Emancipation Proclamation*, which freed slaves in the rebellious Confederacy. But people continued to serve their masters as slaves—in some cases for two and a half more years—because the war raged on, and the truth wasn't made manifest. Slave owners didn't tell their slaves what had happened, and they continued to serve as slaves, although truthfully, they were free.

Likewise, born-again believers have been freed from sin, but not all Christians are experiencing freedom because they don't know who they are and what they have in Christ. Through deception and obscuring the truth, Satan continues to maintain mastery over those who have not yet realized their death and resurrection with Christ. Proverbs 23:7

> In your new, born-again spirit, you are dead to sin.

says, *"For as he thinketh in his heart, so is he."* If you think you're still dead in trespasses and sins while you've also got a new nature, it's only a matter of time until that old nature dominates you again. It's because that is who you think you are.

That shouldn't be the case for any born-again child of God. There's no part of you that is separated from God. If you're born again, your nature has been completely changed! The only thing still compelling you to live the way you did before you got born again is your unrenewed mind (Rom. 12:2). Believers do not have a sinful nature, but if you still believe that you are a sinner by nature, then you'll still let sin influence you.

Don't Be Carnally Minded

For they that are after the flesh do mind the things of the flesh; but they that are after the Spirit the things of the Spirit. For to be carnally minded is death; but to be spiritually minded is *life and peace.*

Romans 8:5–6

Our thoughts control our actions. Notice Paul wrote that carnal-mindedness doesn't just tend toward death—*it is death!* Our lives are going in the direction of our dominant thoughts, so we cannot change our actions without changing our thinking. But you don't just need to change what you think about; you also must change your thinking process. As a part of your soul, your emotions are linked directly to how you think.

The word *carnal* is related to the Spanish word *carne*.[1] You may have eaten or heard of the Spanish dish *chili con carne*, which just means "chili with meat." So, in other words, if you are carnally minded, you're being a meathead! In other words, you're just thinking according to your flesh, and it comes out through your emotions. A lot of this can be found in the misplaced emphasis on self-esteem in the body of Christ.

The secret to victorious Christian living is not found in self-improvement but in self-denial so that Christ can live through us. This does not mean that God wants us to have a bad self-image. It just depends on which self we are talking about. Remember, a born-again believer becomes a new person in Christ. And that's our new identity—we are made righteous in Him!

> Our thoughts control our actions.

The old man is corrupt and incapable of living the Christian life. If the problem is within myself, then there is hope; because through Christ, I can change.

This is freedom. Regardless of what others do or say, I can prosper through Christ.

As a born-again believer, you must put an end to your carnal self-esteem. Don't rely on the supposedly positive attributes of your personality. You have to die to your old self with all its good and bad qualities and walk in your new identity in Christ.

How can you tell if your thoughts and emotions are coming from the new, born-again self or the old carnal self? God's Word is the key. Jesus says in John 6:63,

> *It is the spirit that quickeneth; the flesh prof-iteth nothing: the words that I speak unto you,* they *are spirit, and* they *are life.*

Any thought or emotion that agrees with what God's Word says about you is from the Holy Spirit through your new man. Any thought or emotion that violates God's Word is from the devil through your old man.

If you are in strife with someone (James 3:16), you're acting in the flesh (the old man). Just repent and get back in the spirit (the new man) where you have love, joy, and peace (Gal. 5:22). Similarly, if you are afraid, you're in the flesh.

For God hath not given us the spirit of fear; but of power, and of love, and of a sound mind.

2 Timothy 1:7

Instead of going to God and asking Him to remove the fear, just step out of your natural way of thinking (the flesh) and into the spirit where there is no fear (1 John 4:18). Focus on your "Christ-esteem" (your identity in Him) rather than your self-esteem.

Whose Righteousness?

And if by grace, then is it no more of works: otherwise grace is no more grace. But if it be of works, then is it no more grace: otherwise work is no more work.

Romans 11:6

The word *righteousness* has become a religious cliché and lost its meaning to many people. Even Christians are confused about what righteousness is and how to receive it. This has left our society without a clear understanding of what it takes to have a relationship with God and is reflected in our nation's moral collapse. So, it's imperative that we get back to the basics of righteousness.

A layman's definition of righteousness is simply, "right standing with God." Righteousness is the condition of being in right relationship with the Lord. And this can only happen through total faith and dependence upon Christ. There is no other way, and there is nothing we can add to our faith to obtain right relationship.

One of the things that blinds people to a true understanding of righteousness is confusion about how we become right in the sight of God. It is commonly thought that our actions are the determining factor in God's judgment of our righteousness. That's not true. There is a relationship between our actions and our right standing with God, but right relationship with

God produces actions, not the other way around. That is to say, we are not made righteous by what we do.

Righteousness is a gift that the Lord gives to those who accept what Jesus has done for them (Rom. 5:17–18). Our own actions cannot change our hearts. The gift of salvation produces a changed heart that, in turn, changes our actions. God looks upon the heart of man (1 Sam. 16:7), and we must be righteous in our hearts to truly worship Him (John 4:24).

Thinking that doing what's right makes us righteous is a mistake and the same error the Pharisees made. Religion has always preached that if we clean up our actions, our hearts will become clean too. Jesus taught just the opposite (Matt. 23:25–26). It's through a changed heart that our actions change. The heart is the issue. Actions are only an indication of what is in our hearts.

The Gospel changes hearts. Once hearts are changed, actions change. Once believers start recognizing who they are in Christ, they will start acting truly righteously. Instead of doing good works to please God, they will minister to others because God is already pleased with them according to what Jesus has done.

That means we don't receive righteousness because we deserve it. We get what Jesus deserved because He took what we deserved: judgment. Contrary to popular belief, Christianity does not promote receiving justice from the Lord. Praise God for that! The Lord had a much better plan.

> Righteousness is a gift.

Justice vs. Mercy

All we like sheep have gone astray; we have turned every one to his own way; and the Lord hath laid on him the iniquity of us all.

Isaiah 53:6

I once had a job developing pictures in a photography studio. Some of the customers would come into the studio to look at their proofs and say things like, "This picture doesn't do me justice." I never had the nerve to say this, but I often thought, *You don't need justice, you need mercy!*

That's the way it is with God. We sometimes call for justice, but that's not what we need. The wonderful plan of salvation is that those who put their faith in Jesus and what He did for us get what He deserves. On the other hand, those who do not put their total faith in Christ will ultimately get what *they* deserve. Believe me, that is not what they want. Religion has subtly instructed people to trust in their own goodness instead of God's, and that will never work.

If we were weighed in the balances against God's righteousness, we would come up short. God's righteousness is always more in quantity and quality than ours will ever be. Our righteousness is as filthy rags compared to God's righteousness (Isa. 64:6).

You may be thinking, *That's not fair. No one can compete with God's righteousness.* That's the point! God's righteousness is the standard by which everyone must be measured. Maybe you're thinking, *So then, how can anyone be saved?* The answer is that no one can be saved if they are trusting in their own righteousness. We all must have a righteousness that exceeds anything we could ever produce through our own effort.

Jesus was in right relationship with God like no one else can be. He is the Son of God. *"And without controversy great is the mystery of godliness: God was manifest in the flesh, justified in the Spirit, seen of angels, preached unto the Gentiles, believed on in the world, received up into glory"* (1 Tim. 3:16). He is holy and pure and without sin, yet He became sin for us (2 Cor. 5:21) through no wrongdoing on His part. He took our sin in His own body on the cross (1 Pet. 2:24).

> *Surely he hath borne our griefs, and carried our sorrows: yet we did esteem him stricken, smitten of God, and afflicted. But he* was *wounded for our transgressions,* he was *bruised for our iniquities: the chastisement of our peace* was *upon him; and with his stripes we are healed.*
>
> Isaiah 53:4–5

In return for Jesus taking our sin, born-again believers get His righteousness instead of their own. It's not our actions that make us acceptable to the Father. Our trust in Jesus is what imparts His righteousness into your born-again spirit and puts you in right standing with God.

Know Who You Are

For with the heart man believeth unto righteousness; and with the mouth confession is made unto salvation.

Romans 10:10

The first step in walking in righteousness is knowledge of God's Word. Romans 10:14 says, *"How shall they believe in him of whom they have not heard?"* Verse 17 says, *"So then faith cometh by hearing, and hearing by the word of God."* If we don't know what the Word of God says about who we are in our spirits, it

> Jesus was in right relationship with God like no one else can be.

will be impossible to believe and act accordingly in faith.

Philemon 1:6 says, *"That the communication of thy faith may become effectual by the acknowledging of every good thing which is in you in Christ Jesus."* This verse makes it clear that your faith starts working by knowing the good things in your spirit. You could turn that verse around but keep its meaning by saying, "If you don't know who you are in your spirit man, your faith won't work." And if your faith doesn't work, you cannot access all the benefits of being the righteousness of God in Christ.

The religious teaching that most people receive has left them with the impression that there isn't any good thing in them. They've been taught that the way to activate the power of God in their lives is to keep their unworthiness and weaknesses continually before them, which is basically false humility. They may say things like, "Without Jesus, I can do nothing," which is totally true, but it is not balanced by the truth that *"I can do all things through Christ which strengtheneth me*" (Phil. 4:13). The balanced truth is that I'm never without Jesus in my born-again spirit.

It's like when a person gets up in front of the church to sing a special song and says, "I don't sing very well, but I'd like to make a joyful noise unto the Lord. Please pray for me." Then, when the music starts and they begin to sing, they sound like they were classically trained. Afterward, when somebody tries to compliment them, the person says, "On, no! It wasn't me. It was all Jesus!"

That sounds really good in the moment, but that's typical false humility. Just imagine if you saw that same person at the grocery store later that week and said, "You were right! You sounded terrible!" How do you think that person would react without a church audience around? I bet you'd find out just how humble they really were!

It's true we need to realize that we are totally dependent on Jesus, but we have to go beyond that. Before anything else, we have to realize who we are in our born-again spirits. Because we depend on Jesus, we are totally superior to any weapon the devil can use against us. We are world overcomers (1 John 5:4).

Hebrews 12:2 says we have to look unto Jesus, *"the author and finisher of* our *faith."* But instead, most of us have been looking at ourselves. It's no wonder we've been weary and have fainted in the battle (Heb. 12:3). As we change our attention from our own frailty to Christ's sufficiency and take our place in Him, our faith will be activated.

The Faith of the Son of God

I am crucified with Christ: nevertheless I live; yet not I, but Christ liveth in me: and the life which I now live in the flesh I live by the faith of the Son of God, who loved me, and gave himself for me.

Galatians 2:20

The apostle Paul did not say that he lived by faith *in* the Son of God but by the faith *of* the Son of God. Paul's measure of faith was the same measure that Jesus had. It was Jesus' faith. And Romans 12:3b says, *"God hath dealt to every man the measure of faith."* God didn't give us different measures of faith; we all received *the* measure of faith. If there is only one measure of faith (Rom. 12:3), then believers today also have the faith of Jesus. It's part of our new identity in Christ.

One of the misunderstandings about faith that gives people the most trouble is that they think they have to acquire more faith and that some people have much faith, while others have virtually none. We spend a lot of effort, like a dog chasing its tail, trying to get something we already have. Every born-again Christian already has the same quality and quantity of faith that Jesus has. Once you receive God's supernatural faith at salvation, it doesn't leave you. It is permanently deposited in your born-again spirit.

> *But the fruit of the Spirit is love, joy, peace, long-suffering, gentleness, goodness, **faith**, meekness, temperance: against such there is no law.*
>
> Galatians 5:22–23

There is no lack of faith within any true Christian. There is just a lack of knowing and using what God has already given us. If I were serving soup to people, and if I used the same ladle to dish it out, then that ladle would be the measure of soup. Everyone would get the same amount of soup because I would use the same measure. That's the way it is with God's faith. He only used one measure. All born-again Christians received the same amount of faith—the same amount as Jesus!

Since we have the same faith Jesus has, we can do the same works that Jesus did if we receive this truth and begin to use the faith we have (John 14:12). Faith brings the things God has provided for you from your born-again spirit into the physical realm (Heb. 11:1), and everything the Lord does for us by grace is accessed through faith.

Most people don't doubt that faith works. Unfortunately, they doubt that they have enough faith to get the job done. If Satan can blind you to this truth, then he can keep you from using the faith you have. The Lord has given us everything we need as part of our new identity in Christ, including faith.

The Mind of Christ

For who hath known the mind of the Lord, that he may instruct him? But we have the mind of Christ.

1 Corinthians 2:16

Our minds are the battleground in the fight to stand on the truth that we are new creatures (2 Cor. 5:17) and that we are the righteousness of God in Christ (2 Cor. 5:21). Your spirit is complete (Eph. 4:24; Col. 2:10), and your body will do what it is told, but your soul (mind, will, and emotions) has the responsibility to choose or exercise free will. So, in that sense, your soul is the master control over your whole person.

We've already seen that the spirit is the driving force for the born-again person, but the soul has the last word because of a person's will. God will not violate our free will. So, how do you get this "mind of Christ" (which you have received in your born-again spirit) functioning in your soulish mind so you can make the right choices? By studying the Word of God—the renewing of your mind (Rom. 12:2).

God's Word is the wisdom of God (Luke 11:49) written down so that your soul can read it. But just acknowledging God's Word is not enough (2 Cor. 3:6). You must have spiritual understanding because God's Word is spirit, and it is life (John 6:63).

When the knowledge of God's Word enters your mind through hearing or studying, your born-again spirit bears witness with the truth and imparts wisdom, which is the ability to apply knowledge. Then it becomes revelation (divinely quickened) knowledge—not just facts about God. This explains why the Word of God seems to work for some people and not for others. You may be sitting next to someone in a church service, listening to the same message, and even though it comes alive on the inside of you, it does absolutely nothing for them.

How does the Word of God become alive and powerful in our lives as Hebrews 4:12 talks about? One important way is by meditating on God's Word. Too many times, we get so hungry to learn God's Word that we don't spend enough time for our renewed spirit man to fully disclose the power that is in those words.

There was a time in my life when I was so busy going to hear preachers, the Lord told me to focus on Him and make the truth of His Word a reality in my own life. It had to become a revelation to me before the Lord's power really began to work consistently. You would be better off with only a small amount of true revelation from the Word in you than if you had vast amounts of Scripture with just a carnal understanding.

This revelation knowledge is what has been missing in religion's approach to God's Word. Carnal preachers have been putting out carnal knowledge to carnal people, and therefore, the true power of God's Word has not been released.

Spirit, Soul, and Body

And the very God of peace sanctify you wholly; and I pray God *your whole spirit and soul and body be preserved blameless unto the coming of our Lord Jesus Christ.*

1 Thessalonians 5:23

Let's go back to the story when the Lord really touched my life on March 23, 1968. All those tangible feelings of God's love I had been experiencing eventually wore off, and I committed myself to studying God's Word.

Although I was laying a foundation by studying the Bible, I was still perplexed by how such a holy, pure God could love someone like me. I didn't doubt His love because I had experienced it. I just didn't understand how He could love and show kindness to me when I knew I didn't deserve it. That's when I came across 2 Corinthians 5:17. That verse said I was a new creature and that old things had passed away, but I just couldn't embrace it.

I knew I was in Christ, but it seemed like my old self was still in place, and there were many things that hadn't passed away. I was still confused, fearful, and very unsure of myself. I was still an introvert and found it very hard to talk to people I wasn't already friends with. It seemed like I constantly failed God. I just couldn't see this "new creature" when I looked at myself in the mirror. Then the Holy Spirit led me to 1 Thessalonians 5:23.

I saw that I had only known myself in the body and the soulish realms. But there was a third part of me that I wasn't aware of—the part that was now like Christ. Although I couldn't see or feel my born-again spirit, I had to just accept what God's Word said about who I was—identical to Christ (1 John 4:17). That was my true identity!

Jesus said,

The words that I speak unto you, they are spirit, and they are life.

John 6:63b

According to James, God's Word is like looking in a spiritual mirror (James 1:22–25). If you want to see your face, you have to look in a physical mirror. No one can see their face directly with their eyes. Likewise, you can't see your spirit with your eyes, but you can believe what the spiritual mirror of God's Word says about you and act accordingly. When I "saw" this, it finally helped me realize who I truly was in Christ.

Not long after the Lord touched my life on March 23, 1968, I said, "Lord, I'm just going to believe what your Word says even though I'm not seeing it." So, I stood in front of a mirror, eyeball to eyeball with myself, pointed my finger at my reflection, and said, "Andrew, you are the righteousness of God in Christ!" And when I said that, all the hair stood up on the back of my neck. I was waiting for a lightning bolt to strike and turn me into a pile of ashes. But that's what the Word said about me. I had to accept what God said about me in the spiritual mirror of the Bible and start saying it by faith to my reflection in the physical mirror.

Hearing myself say that stirred up my faith because Romans 10:17 says,

So then faith cometh *by hearing, and hearing by the word of God.*

It's one thing to hear a minister say it to you, but when you say it about yourself, it affects you in a deeper way. I had to start speaking to myself that I was the righteousness of God in Christ, and after a while, I began to believe it!

Raising-the-Dead Power

Early on in our ministry, my heart longed to see the dead raised. Through my born-again spirit, I already had raising-the-dead power on the inside of me (Eph. 1:18–20). But in order to really see it manifest in my ministry, I had to renew my mind to the truth of God's Word. So I went through the Bible, studied every time someone was raised from the dead, and then meditated on it until I saw myself (in my imagination) raising people from the dead just like Jesus did.

When I was a pastor in Pritchett, Colorado, there was a paraplegic man I would visit who was paralyzed from the waist down. I was at his house every day to pray for and minister to him. Previously unable to move, I'd helped him move his legs, get around, and do things. Then one evening, while I was preparing to start a service at the local church, this man's son came in and waved me down. When I walked over, he threw me—and my guitar—into his car and drove us the short distance to his parents' house.

I just thought we were going to pray for his father—that maybe he was in some pain. But as I walked in, the sheriff was there with some emergency equipment; and the man's wife was crying and praying, "O God, please bring him back from the dead!" That was the first time I realized he was dead.

Since I already had so much time and effort invested in this man and his healing, the first thought that came to me was, "No way!" So, I walked over to him and said, "In the name of Jesus, come back into that body." All of a sudden, he just sat straight up! Later, a doctor checked him out and confirmed what had happened.

Now, if I was in a church service and shared that story, then asked everyone if they believed someone could be raised from the dead, the majority of the crowd may stand up and shout, "Yes! Amen!" But if someone fell over dead in the church, and I pointed to the congregation and said, "Now, one of you come up here and raise this person from the dead," I guarantee there wouldn't be as many people excited over it.

That's because in those situations, people don't look to their new identity in Christ. They believe Jesus, an apostle, or even some minister could raise someone from the dead. But they'd think about how sinful or unworthy they are. In other words, they'd see themselves according to that old, dead sin nature and not as a new creature or the righteousness of God in Christ.

Over the years, I've seen multiple people raised from the dead—including my own wife and son. It wasn't because of anything special about me. Throughout my whole life, I've been average. But I don't let those thoughts keep me from ministering the power of God that's in me. I know from the Word of God who I am in my spirit—I know my true identity— and that's the place I minister from. And, because God is no respecter of persons (Acts 10:34; Rom. 2:11), you can too!

Conclusion

Remember the concept of looking at yourself in the mirror (James 1:22–25)? We need to see ourselves by who we are in Christ not in the way the mirror looks in the natural. In the natural, you may not look like much, but in your spirit, you are absolutely awesome and anointed by God! You've got to be able to see yourself this way.

My attitude completely changed when I discovered the truths I've shared in this booklet. When problems came, I used to feel inadequate. I'd pray, "Oh God, I know You've got power, but I'm just a man. I don't have any power of my own." Then I realized I'm not just a man anymore. I am a new creation, and I am the righteousness of God in Christ. Because of the confidence, security, and faith this has given me, I can confront and overcome problems because I know who I am in Christ.

FURTHER STUDY

If you enjoyed this booklet and would like to learn more about some of the things I've shared, I suggest my teachings:

- *Spirit, Soul, and Body*
- *My Appointment with God*
- *You've Already Got It!*
- *Romans: Paul's Masterpiece on Grace*
- *The War Is Over*
- *The Old Man Is Dead*

These teachings are available for free at **awmi.net**, or they can be purchased at **awmi.net/store**.

Receive Jesus as Your Savior

Choosing to receive Jesus Christ as your Lord and Savior is the most important decision you'll ever make!

God's Word promises, *"That if thou shalt confess with thy mouth the Lord Jesus, and shalt believe in thine heart that God hath raised him from the dead, thou shalt be saved. For with the heart man believeth unto righteousness; and with the mouth confession is made unto salvation"* (Rom. 10:9–10). *"For whosoever shall call upon the name of the Lord shall be saved"* (Rom. 10:13). By His grace, God has already done everything to provide salvation. Your part is simply to believe and receive.

Pray out loud: "Jesus, I acknowledge that I've sinned and need to receive what you did for the forgiveness of my sins. I confess that You are my Lord and Savior. I believe in my heart that God raised You from the dead. By faith in Your Word, I receive salvation now. Thank You for saving me."

The very moment you commit your life to Jesus Christ, the truth of His Word instantly comes to pass in your spirit. Now that you're born again, there's a brand-new you!

Please contact us and let us know that you've prayed to receive Jesus as your Savior. We'd like to send you some free materials to help you on your new journey. Call our Helpline: **719-635-1111** (available 24 hours a day, seven days a week) to speak to a staff member who is here to help you understand and grow in your new relationship with the Lord.

Welcome to your new life!

Receive the Holy Spirit

As His child, your loving heavenly Father wants to give you the supernatural power you need to live a new life. *"For every one that asketh receiveth; and he that seeketh findeth; and to him that knocketh it shall be opened… how much more shall* your *heavenly Father give the Holy Spirit to them that ask him?"* (Luke 11:10–13).

All you have to do is ask, believe, and receive! Pray this: "Father, I recognize my need for Your power to live a new life. Please fill me with Your Holy Spirit. By faith, I receive it right now. Thank You for baptizing me. Holy Spirit, You are welcome in my life."

Some syllables from a language you don't recognize will rise up from your heart to your mouth (1 Cor. 14:14). As you speak them out loud by faith, you're releasing God's power from within and building yourself up in the spirit (1 Cor. 14:4). You can do this whenever and wherever you like.

It doesn't really matter whether you felt anything or not when you prayed to receive the Lord and His Spirit. If you believed in your heart that you received, then God's Word promises you did. *"Therefore I say unto you, What things soever ye desire, when ye pray, believe that ye receive* them, *and ye shall have* them" (Mark 11:24). God always honors His Word—believe it!

We would like to rejoice with you, pray with you, and answer any questions to help you understand more fully what has taken place in your life!

Please contact us to let us know that you've prayed to be filled with the Holy Spirit and to request the book *The New You & the Holy Spirit*. This book will explain in more detail about the benefits of being filled with the Holy Spirit and speaking in tongues. Call our Helpline: **719-635-1111** (available 24 hours a day, seven days a week).

Call for Prayer

If you need prayer for any reason, you can call our Helpline, 24 hours a day, seven days a week at **719-635-1111**. A trained prayer minister will answer your call and pray with you.

Every day, we receive testimonies of healings and other miracles from our Helpline, and we are ministering God's nearly-too-good-to-be-true message of the Gospel to more people than ever. So, I encourage you to call today!

About the Author

Andrew Wommack's life was forever changed the moment he encountered the supernatural love of God on March 23, 1968. As a renowned Bible teacher and author, Andrew has made it his mission to change the way the world sees God.

Andrew's vision is to go as far and deep with the Gospel as possible. His message goes far through the *Gospel Truth* television program, which is available to over half the world's population. The message goes deep through discipleship at Charis Bible College, headquartered in Woodland Park, Colorado. Founded in 1994, Charis has campuses across the United States and around the globe.

Andrew also has an extensive library of teaching materials in print, audio, and video. More than 200,000 hours of free teachings can be accessed at **awmi.net**.

Contact Information

Andrew Wommack Ministries, Inc.

PO Box 3333
Colorado Springs, CO 80934-3333
info@awmi.net
awmi.net

Helpline: 719-635-1111 (available 24/7)

Charis Bible College

info@charisbiblecollege.org
844-360-9577
CharisBibleCollege.org

For a complete list of all of our offices,
visit **awmi.net/contact-us**.

Connect with us on social media.

Andrew's LIVING COMMENTARY BIBLE SOFTWARE

Andrew Wommack's *Living Commentary* Bible study software is a user-friendly, downloadable program. It's like reading the Bible with Andrew at your side, sharing his revelation with you verse by verse.

Main features:
- Bible study software with a grace-and-faith perspective
- Over 26,000 notes by Andrew on verses from Genesis through Revelation
- *Matthew Henry's Concise Commentary*
- 12 Bible versions
- 2 concordances: *Englishman's Concordance* and *Strong's Concordance*
- 2 dictionaries: *Collaborative International Dictionary* and *Holman's Dictionary*
- Atlas with biblical maps
- Bible and *Living Commentary* statistics
- Quick navigation, including history of verses
- Robust search capabilities (for the Bible and Andrew's notes)
- "Living" (i.e., constantly updated and expanding)
- Ability to create personal notes

Whether you're new to studying the Bible or a seasoned Bible scholar, you'll gain a deeper revelation of the Word from a grace-and-faith perspective.

Purchase Andrew's *Living Commentary* today at **awmi.net/living**, and grow in the Word with Andrew.

Item code: 8350

ANDREW WOMMACK MINISTRIES

CHARIS
BIBLE COLLEGE

God has more for you.

Are you longing to find your God-given purpose? At Charis Bible College you will establish a firm foundation in the Word of God and receive hands-on ministry experience to **find, follow,** and **fulfill** your purpose.

Scan the QR code for a free Charis teaching!

CharisBibleCollege.org
Admissions@awmcharis.com
(844) 360-9577

Change your life. **Change the world.**

Made in United States
Troutdale, OR
05/03/2024

19626644R00040